First Time

Going to
the Dentist

Melinda Beth Radabaugh

Heinemann Library

Chicago, Illinois

Customer Service 888-454-2279
Visit our website at www.heinemannlibrary.com

Designed by Sue Emerson, Heinemann Library; Page layout by Que-Net Media™
Printed and bound in the United States by Lake Book Manufacturing, Inc.
Photo research by Janet Lankford-Moran

08 07 06 05 04
10 9 8 7 6 5 4 3 2 1

Library of Congress Cataloging-in-Publication Data
Radabaugh, Melinda Beth.
  Going to the dentist / Melinda Beth Radabaugh.
      v. cm. – (First time)
Contents: What is a dentist? – Why do you go to the dentist? – Where do you see the dentist? – What happens at the dentist's office? – What does the dentist do? – Who helps the dentist? – What tools does the dentist use? – What do you learn? – What happens next?
  ISBN 1-4034-0228-0 (HC) 1-4034-0467-4 (Pbk.)
  1. Children–Preparation for dental care–Juvenile literature. [1. Dental care. 2. Dentists.] I. Title. II. Series.
  RK63.R33 2003
  617.6–dc21

                                    2002155331

Acknowledgments
The author and publishers are grateful to the following for permission to reproduce copyright material:
p. 4 Joe Carini/Index Stock Imagery, Inc.; p. 5 Taxi/Getty Images; p. 6 Brian Warling Studio/Heinemann Library; pp. 7, 13 Stone/Getty Images; pp. 8, 11, 16, 17, 18, 19, 21 Robert Lifson/Heinemann Library; p. 9 Oijoy Photography/Heinemann Library; p. 10 Tom Stewart/Corbis; p. 12 Mark Richards/Photo Edit Inc.; p. 14 Ariel Skelley/Corbis; p. 15 Johner/Photonica; p. 20 Corbis; p. 22 (column 1, T-B) Corbis, PhotoDisc, Robert Lifson/Heinemann Library; (column 2) Corbis; p. 23 (row 1, L-R) Mark Richards/Photo Edit Inc., Corbis, Robert Lifson/Heinemann Library; (row 2, L-R) Brian Warling Studio/Heinemann Library, Robert Lifson/Heinemann Library, Robert Lifson/Heinemann Library; (row 3, L-R) Robert Lifson/Heinemann Library, Tom Stewart/Corbis, Corbis; (row 4) PhotoDisc; p. 24 (column 1) Corbis, Robert Lifson/Heinemann Library; (column 2) Corbis; back cover (L-R) Robert Lifson/Heinemann Library, PhotoDisc

Cover photograph by Taxi/Getty Images

Every effort has been made to contact copyright holders of any material reproduced in this book. Any omissions will be rectified in subsequent printings if notice is given to the publisher.

Special thanks to our advisory panel for their help in the preparation of this book:

Alice Bethke, Library Consultant
Palo Alto, CA

Eileen Day, Preschool Teacher
Chicago, IL

Kathleen Gilbert,
Second Grade Teacher
Round Rock, TX

Sandra Gilbert,
Library Media Specialist
Fiest Elementary School
Houston, TX

Jan Gobeille,
Kindergarten Teacher
Garfield Elementary
Oakland, CA

Angela Leeper,
Educational Consultant
Wake Forest, NC

Special thanks to Dr. Jessica L. Bishop, DDS, for her help in reviewing this book.

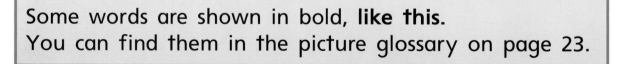

Some words are shown in bold, **like this.**
You can find them in the picture glossary on page 23.

Contents

What Is a Dentist?

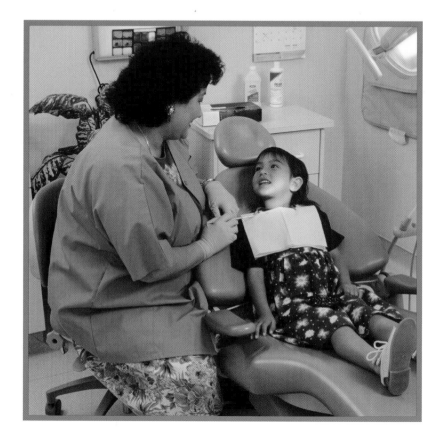

A dentist is someone who takes care of teeth.

Dentists can fix hurt teeth.

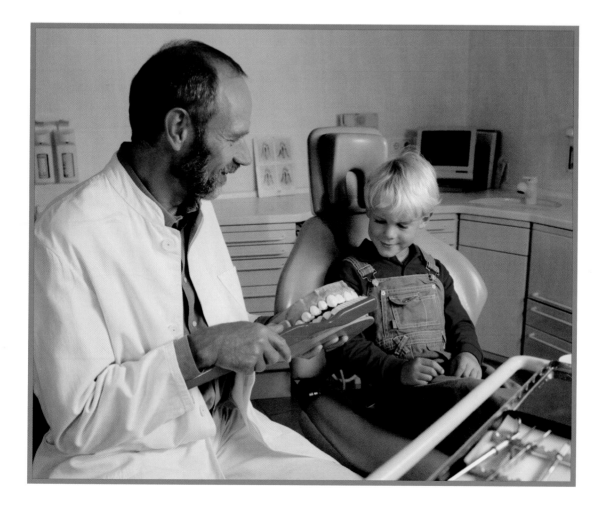

Dentists use tools to check teeth.

They teach you to care for
your teeth.

Why Do You Go to the Dentist?

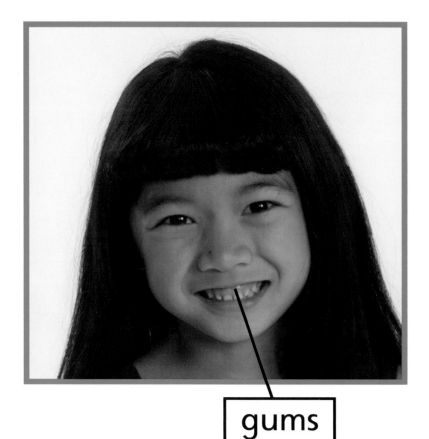

gums

You go to the dentist to get a checkup.

A checkup keeps your teeth and **gums** healthy.

6

You go if you have a hurt tooth.

Where Do Dentists Work?

A dentist works in an **office**.

The office might be in a big building.

The office might be in a house.

What Happens at the Dentist's Office?

receptionist

A **receptionist** is the first person you see.

She helps you sign in.

Then, you wait in the waiting room.

Sometimes you can play with
toys or read a book there.

What Happens Next?

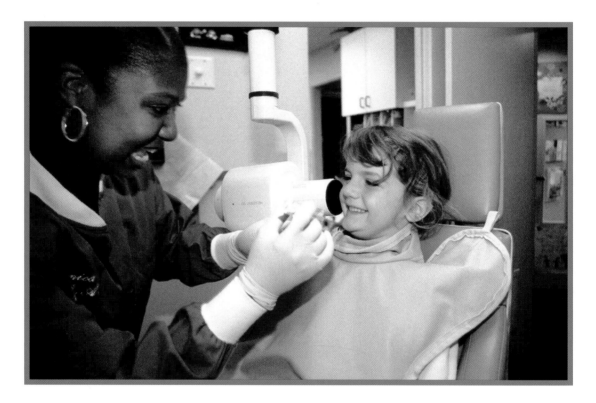

An **assistant** takes **X rays** of your teeth.

X rays are pictures that help the dentist see your teeth.

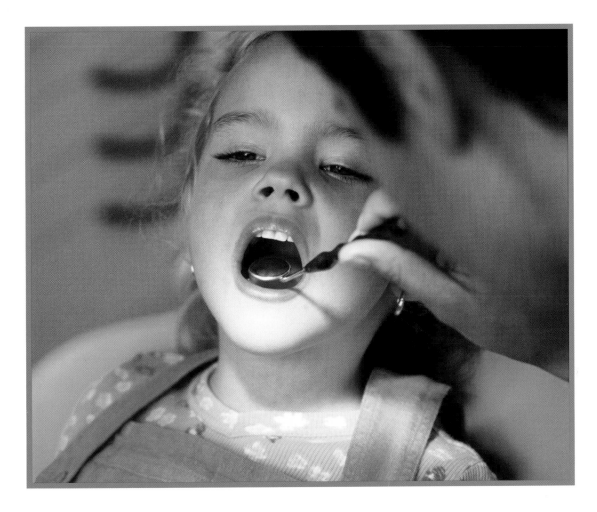

Then, the dentist looks inside your mouth.

Dentists use a special mirror to help them see.

What Happens During a Checkup?

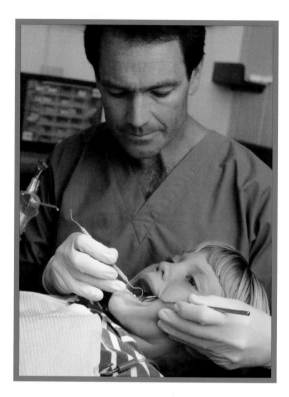

Dentists count and touch your teeth with a special tool called a **probe.**

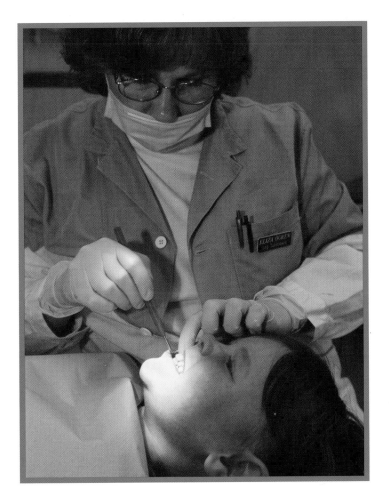

The dentist feels your teeth and **gums.**

This is to make sure they are healthy.

What Does a Hygienist Do?

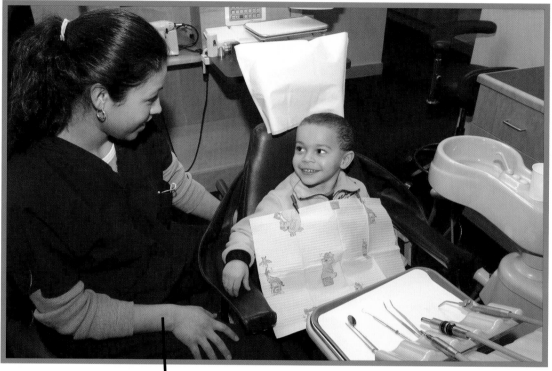

hygienist

A **hygienist** cleans your teeth.

She cleans your teeth with a special toothbrush.

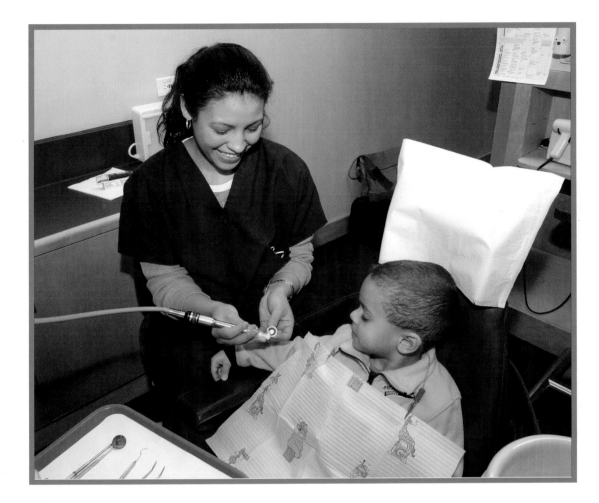

The hygienist uses special **toothpaste** to clean your teeth.

The **electric toothbrush** tickles!

What Happens After the Checkup?

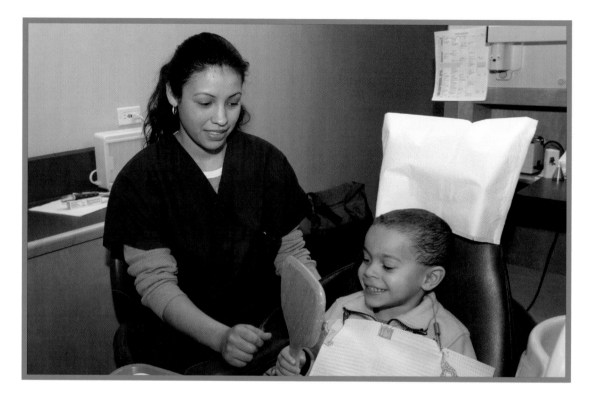

You look in the mirror.

Now, your teeth are clean and shiny.

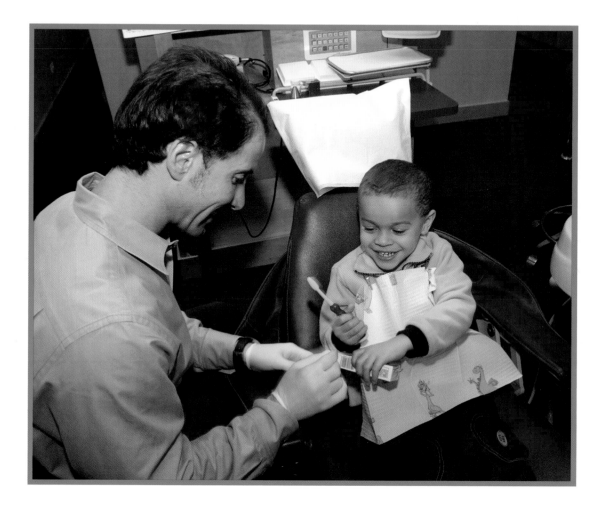

You get a new toothbrush and **toothpaste!**

Then, you can leave to go home.

What Do You Learn?

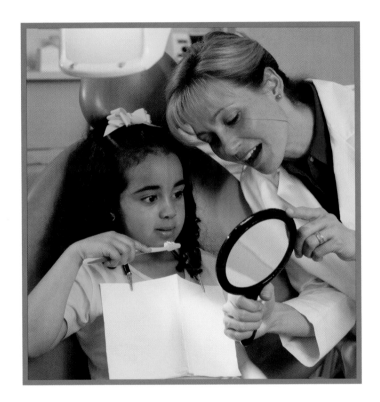

You learn how to brush your teeth.

You practice with a toothbrush.

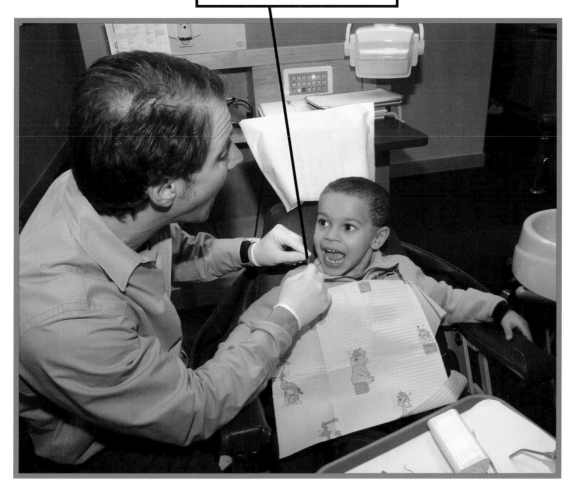

dental floss

You also learn to use **dental floss.**

You can floss at home, too!

Quiz

What can you find at the dentist's **office?**

Look for the answer on page 24.

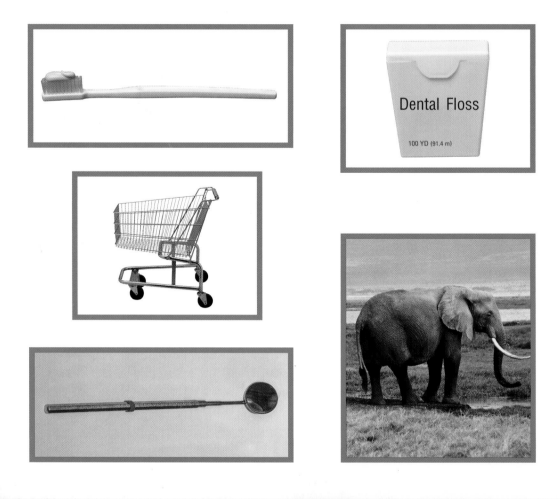

Picture Glossary

assistant
page 12

hygienist
(hi-JEN-ist)
pages 16, 17

receptionist
(ree-SEP-shun-ist)
page 10

dental floss
page 21

office
pages 8, 9

toothpaste
pages 17, 19

electric toothbrush
page 17

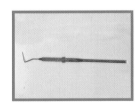
probe
page 14

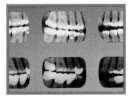
X ray
page 12

gums
pages 6, 15

Note to Parents and Teachers

Reading for information is an important part of a child's literacy development. Learning begins with a question about something. Help children think of themselves as investigators and researchers by encouraging their questions about the world around them. Each chapter in this book begins with a question. Read the question together. Look at the pictures. Talk about what you think the answer might be. Then read the text to find out if your predictions were correct. Think of other questions you could ask about the topic, and discuss where you might find the answers. Assist children in using the picture glossary and the index to practice new vocabulary and research skills.

Index

Answer to quiz on page 22

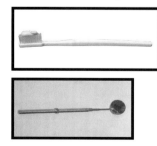

You can find the toothbrush, the dental floss, and the mirror at the dentist's office.